ST. PHILIP
& THE APOSTLES
of the
FATHER

Answering the Call
To Know, Love and Honor
God Your Father

DR. THOMAS W. PETRISKO

ST. ANDREW'S
PRODUCTIONS

© 2016 St. Andrew's Productions

All rights reserved. No part of this book may be produced in any manner without permission in writing from the publisher.

ISBN: 978-1-891903-46-5

Published by:
St. Andrew's Productions
PO Box 54204
Pittsburgh, PA   15244
Tel: 412-787-9735
Fax: 412-787-5204
Web: saintandrew.com
Email: standrewsproductions@yahoo.com

Special thanks to Ignatius Press, Alba House, Queenship Publishing, Random House and all other publishers for permission to quote from their works.

The author and publisher are grateful to those publishers of others whose materials, whether in the public domain or protected by copyright laws, have been used in one form or another in this book. Every reasonable effort has been made to determine copyright holders of excerpted material and photographs and to secure permissions as needed. If any copyrighted materials have been inadvertently used in this work without proper credit being given in one form or another, please notify the Publisher in writing so that future printings of this work may be corrected accordingly.

COVER ARTWORK
The cover design and layout are by Deborah Perdue of Illumination Graphics of Grants Pass, Oregon.

PRINTED IN THE UNITED STATES OF AMERICA

AVAILABLE TO SPEAK

Dr. Thomas W. Petrisko is available to come to your Church or organization to speak about God the Father's great love for mankind and His call for His children to return to Him. He is also available for radio, television, internet and print media interviews. If you desire to contact him, please call: (412)-787-9735 or contact St. Andrew's Productions at www.saintandrew.com

IN APPRECIATION

Once more, I am especially thankful of my wife, Emily, and to my six children, Maria, Sarah, Joshua, Natasha, Dominique and Jesse. No words can express my love for them and my appreciation of their support for this work.

SPECIAL THANKS

I wish to thank my editors, Dr. Frank Novasack, Jr., Erica Rankin, Maria Petrisko and Michael Fontecchio. I am also grateful to Fr. William McCarthy, Fr. David Tourville, Mary Lou Sokol and Amanda DeFazio for their prayers, words and assistance.

SCRIPTURAL CREDITS

Scriptural quotations are taken from the Holy Bible – RSV: Catholic Edition. Alternate translations from the Latin Vulgate Bible (Douay Rheims Version – DV) are indicated when used. Some of the Scriptural quotations are from the New American Bible, the New American Bible – St. Joseph Edition, the New American Bible – Fireside Family Edition 1984-195, the Douay Rheims Bible, the New American Bible – Red Letter Edition 1986, the New Jerusalem Bible, The New Jerusalem Bible 1966, The Douay Rheims Old Testament of the Holy Catholic Bible, 1992.

DEDICATION

This book is dedicated to Fr. William McCarthy, whose support and encouragement has never waivered over the past three decades. A true apostle of our Father, he is an inspiration to all who know him, one of God the Father's chosen ones whose work and words will remain with us long after he has returned to the House of the Father.

AUTHOR'S NOTE

Some of contents of this book have been excerpted from two of my other books: *The Mystery of the Divine Paternal Heart of God Our Father* and *Living in the Heart of the Father*. To order these books, please contact **St. Andrew's Productions at (412)-787-9735** or email standrewsproductions@yahoo.com . The web address is: *saintandrew.com*

CONTENTS

INTRODUCTION 1

CHAPTER ONE – ST. PHILIP AND THE FATHER 9

CHAPTER TWO – CONSECRATION TO OUR FATHER 15

CHAPTER THREE –
A LADDER TO OUR FATHER'S HEART 23

CHAPTER FOUR –
THE SOLEMNITY OF THE DIVINE PATERNAL HEART. 31

CHAPTER FIVE –
THE FEAST OF THE FATHER OF ALL MANKIND 35

CHAPTER SIX – THE CELEBRATION OF LIFE 43

CHAPTER SEVEN –
RAISING OUR VOICES TO THE FATHER. 49

CHAPTER EIGHT –
APOSTLES OF THE FATHER 53

NOTES 60

INTRODUCTION

"No one has even seen God; it is the only Son, who is nearest to the Father's Heart, who has made him known" (Jn 1-18).

In his apostolic letter, *Tertio Millennio Adveniente*, St. John Paul II wrote that "the whole of the Christian life is like a *great pilgrimage to the house of the Father*, whose unconditional love for every human creature, and in particular for the 'prodigal son' (Lk 15:11-32), we discover anew each day." In this same apostolic letter he also reminded us that during this time, Mary, our Mother, will be lovingly and urgently inviting "all the children of God, so that they will return to the house of the Father when they hear her maternal voice: **'Do whatever Christ tells you.'** (Jn 2:5)"

Our return to our Father, then, is ordained by God as a "process." It is a process that begins with our Mother Mary who tenderly guides us to her Son. Jesus then mercifully lifts us upon His Cross to our Father. While comforting us on this journey home, the Holy Spirit purifies and refines us so God our Father can come and dwell in us as living temples, And we, in turn, can dwell in Him.

To do this, we must offer our unconditional *"Yes"* to our Father's will.

THE DIVINE PATERNAL HEART

Now, in our time, the Father shows us the means to approach Him the way He desires most in order to hasten our journey back to Him – it is through His Heart, His *Divine Paternal Heart*.

It is the Heart He wants all to come to know, see, and love, for it is the Heart that created the universe out of love.

It is the Heart, that out of love, created mankind, each and every soul.

It is the Heart that lives and loves in every line of Scripture, in both the Old and New Testaments.

Most of all, it is the Heart that has been waiting for so long to be discovered and subsequently be loved, so it may then pour out upon mankind its greatest expression of love, which is contained and reserved by our Father in trembling anticipation of His re-unification with all creation – just as it was meant to be from the beginning and the way His Heart designed it.

Depicted so perfectly in Michelangelo's *Creation of Man*, our Father is now ready to reach down to His children, touch their hearts with a new infusion of His love and His life, and to gently pull us out of the *culture of death* that now blankets the world like a dense fog that has seeped into every nation. The light needed to penetrate that fog is the light of our Father, the light emanating from His Paternal Heart, the light that He calls all to see and come to in this time.

While for some this understanding will be new, the theology of this truth has never been hidden; it just has not been fully explored and understood as the Holy Spirit now intends it to be.

Each of us is conceived in the Heart of our Father and each is called, moreover drawn, to return to His Heart. As the Prodigal Son hurried into the arms of his loving and forgiving Father, we are also invited to seek and discover that moment of supreme joy and surrender to our Father's loving embrace, to the warmth and safety of his Paternal Heart. Indeed, we are called to that same spark of awareness, that epiphany that the Prodigal Son experienced as he contemplated relief from the misery of the consequences stemming from his misspent choices. In his heart he knew and remembered his father's great love for him, and set out to return to the source of such undying love: *his father's heart*.

THE CHURCH AND THE HEART OF THE FATHER

As with the Sacred Heart of Jesus and the Immaculate Heart of Mary, the Divine Paternal Heart of God the Father is found in the writings of many of the great Fathers, Doctors, Saints and Popes over the centuries. In the early Church, St. Ambrose wrote of the Heart of the Father, "The Son lives by the Father because He is the Word given forth from the Heart of the Father." Likewise, St. Theophilus, the 6th Bishop of Antioch wrote, "In Paradise the Son is set in the Heart of the Father, conversing with the Father in the Garden over Adam."

Through the years, many great Church figures have written of the Father's Heart. Known for spreading devotions to the Hearts of Jesus and Mary, St. John Eudes wrote, "Return to that most loving Heart of your Father, which is full of love and mercy for you." Similarly, the great theologian of the middles ages, St. Francis de Sales, described in one of his books the mercy of the Father's Paternal Heart, "The chorus of the Church Triumphant and those of the Church Militant are united to our Lord in this divine action, so that with Him, in Him and through Him, they may ravish the Heart of God the Father and make His mercy all our own." Even St. Faustina Kowalska confesses in her book, *Divine Mercy in My Soul*, that as a child the "Father lifted me from the ground to His Heart."

PAPAL STATEMENTS

These writings all point to a great mystery of the faith that is waiting to be explored more fully – the great Paternal love of the Father as symbolized in His Paternal Heart. In recent times, Pope Pius XII, Pope John Paul II, Pope Benedict XVI, and Pope Francis have all written or spoken of the Father's Heart. Pope Pius XII, in his encyclical letter, *Hauretis Aquas*, said the way to the Father's Heart is through the Heart of Jesus. Pope John Paul II, in his great apostolic letter, *Tertio Millennio Adveniente*, said that the Father's Paternal Heart causes Him to be endlessly in search of the return of His children. While Pope Benedict XVI, in his acclaimed book, *Jesus of*

Nazareth, repeatedly referenced that Christ was in the Heart of the Father before all creation and it is this understanding, as found in the *Prologue* of *The Gospel of St. John*, "the Son is nearest the Father's Heart" (Jn 1:18), that is the key to our better understanding as to why Christ is the perfect reflection of the Father.

On January 31, 2016, Pope Francis in his *Angelus Address* at St. Peter's Square said, "God, who is Father takes care of each one of his creatures, even the smallest and most insignificant in the eyes of man. This is precisely what the prophetic meaning of Jesus consists of, announcing that no human condition can constitute grounds for exclusion from the Heart of the Father… "

Even the *Catechism of the Catholic Church* asserts that God's plan for mankind stems from the **"Father's Heart."**

FR. JEAN GALOT

Returning to our Heavenly Father, to His love, to His Paternal Heart is the most profound hunger of the human soul. Fr. Jean Galot, SJ, an eminent biblicist and theologian known for his work in the areas of Christology, teaches at the Pontifical Gregorian University in Rome. In his book, *ABBA, FATHER: We Long to See Your Face (Theological Insights Into the First Person the Trinity)*, he writes that every human heart desires to know the Father, to penetrate His Heart:

> "Only such knowledge of God the Father can fulfill the deepest yearnings of the human heart. As long as God is seen simply as God without a Father's Face, an essential aspect is lacking in the vision of the one who

hopes to encounter Him. The human soul needs the revelation of the Father, and its deepest desires which are inspired and quickened by grace are satisfied only when it discovers God as a Father. That is how, in revealing Himself, the Son reveals the Father: 'No one has ever seen God; the only begotten Son of God – Who is the Bosom of the Father – He has revealed Him' (Jn 1:18). The purpose of this revelation is to plunge us into the *Heart of the Father*, into His intimacy."

CONSECRATION TO OUR FATHER

Total intimacy with our Father, into His Paternal Heart: this is the truth than needs to be illuminated, so our Father's children realize their inheritance, the love our one Father in Heaven has for them and desires to pour out upon souls in a special way.

But our Father's call is more than just an invitation for His children to experience a greater personal relationship with Him. Rather, it is a call to all mankind to return to its Father, to its Creator, so He can shower his love upon us all and heal our broken world, and so we can honor Him in a way that is long overdue.

Accordingly then, from the highest levels of the Church to the pulpits of every parish in every diocese, the call must be proclaimed to the faithful that their Father is anxiously awaiting His children to return to Him – to His Heart – so He can race to meet them and share the mysteries of His divine paternal love, therefore satisfying the deepest yearnings of their hearts to know the Father. As St. Philip said: **"Lord, show us the Father and then we will be satisfied."** (Jn 14:8)

Indeed, the time has come for God's children to return to their Father, to love Him and *consecrate* themselves to Him, and for the world to more profoundly know, love and honor the One Who Christ desired all to know, love and honor – His Father and our Father – the Father of All Mankind.

THE FEAST OF LIFE

Moreover, the Church needs to hear the voice of God's children, their cry of love for their Heavenly Father, by responding with an octave feast, The *Feast of Life*: **The Solemnity of the Divine Paternal Heart, the Feast of the Father of All Mankind!** It is to be a feast that gives our Father all the honor and glory that Scripture tells us He deserves.

Fr. Raniero Cantalamessa, O.F.M. Cap., The *Preacher to the Papal Household* since 1980 under Pope John Paul II, Pope Benedict XVI, and Pope Francis, is a professor, theologian and the author of numerous articles and books. In his writings, Fr. Cantalamessa has called for a feast in the Catholic Church dedicated to God the Father. Fr. Cantalmessa states:

> "Christians would certainly give great joy to the risen Lord if they were able to project "ecumenically," that is, reach an agreement with all the churches who accept it in order to celebrate, with one accord the *Feast of the Father* on the same day. While we look forward to this day, we can already celebrate the *Feast of the Father* "in Spirit and in truth," in the intimacy of our hearts, by perhaps promoting little spiritual initiatives

whose purpose is to make the Father known more, to honor Him and express all our filial love for Him, in union with Jesus, who always celebrates His Father."

Indeed, the joy of finding God, manifested in many religions, as one common Father, would be an inspiration for every person and every heart.

This, then, is the calling to the faithful, especially to those who hear the voice of our Father in a special way. Like St. Philip, we need to want to see the Father so we will be satisfied, so we will come to better know, love and honor Him – so we can give ourselves to the Father with our personal fiat, our *"yes"* to His Paternal Heart.

CHAPTER ONE

ST. PHILIP AND THE FATHER

"Just Father, the world has not known you, but I have known you, and these men have known you sent me. To them I have revealed your name, and I will continue to reveal it, so that your love for me may live in them, and I may live in them" (Jn 17:25-26).

"'Lord,' Phillip said to him, 'show us the Father and that will be enough for us.'
'Philip,' Jesus replied, 'after I have been with you all this time, you still do not know me?'
'Whoever has seen me has seen the Father. How can you say, 'Show us the Father'? Do you not believe that I am in the Father and the Father is in me?
The words I speak are not spoken of myself; it is the Father who lives in me accomplishing his works.

Believe me that I am in the Father
and the Father is in me,
or else, believe because of the works I do.
I solemnly assure you, the man who has faith in me
will do the works I do, and
greater far than these.
Why? Because I go to the Father,
and whatever you ask in my name I will do.
so as to glorify the Father in the Son.
Anything you ask me in my name
I will do.
If you love me
and obey the commands I give you,
I will ask the Father and he will
give you another Paraclete –
to be with you always:
the Spirit of Truth…"

In 1994, I traveled to Mt. Tabor in the Holy Land. It was a highly anticipated and deeply profound experience for me. This is because I had always wondered what it must have been like for the three Apostles – Sts. Peter, John and James – to be there to witness the Transfigured Jesus, to behold the extraordinary vision of Moses and Elijah, and to hear the voice of God the Father: "This is my beloved Son on whom my favor rests. Listen to him."[2]

The experiences of these three individuals come to mind when contemplating which Saint is best associated with God the Father. Who would be a shining and powerful example of devotion to our Father?

ST. PHILIP

As we know, the Father inspired St. Peter to voice his public affirmation that Jesus was the Messiah, the "Son of the living God." St. John the Baptist, like the three Apostles on Mt. Tabor, heard the Father's voice at the Jordan River. There are, of course, numerous holy men and women worthy of consideration. From St. Irenaeus – the *Father of Christian Theology*, whose writings on the Father reveal his profound devotion to "the uncreated, beyond grasp, invisible, Maker of all"[3] – to St. Catherine of Sienna – whose mystical *Dialogue* with God the Father is a classic in Christian literature – there are many Saints that have expressed their strong devotion to God the Father.

But while many names come to mind, I believe that St. Phillip best shows us the way to the Father. For his very words in Scripture ask Christ to do just that:

"Lord, show us the Father and that will be enough for us" (Jn 14:8).

Needless to say, if St. Peter's declaration of Christ being "the Son of the living God" was a result of the Father's revelation to him, St. Phillip's desire for Jesus to "show us the Father" appears to be no less a moment of divine prodding.

THE LAST DISCOURSE

There is a reason for this belief.

In the annals of time, few words may be found to have contributed as much to man's quest to find its Father than Phillip's heartfelt plea to Jesus. This is because Christ, in responding to Phillip, uses the moment at hand to unfold for us what is known as the *Last Discourse*; these were His departing, immortal words to the Apostles in the *Gospel of St. John* that emphasized His mission to lead all back to the Father, so all may be "one" in the Father as He is "one" in the Father.

Jesus explains to His Apostles that through love of the Father, man is invited to intimately know and share in the very *life in God*. In the *Last Discourse*, which runs from Chapter 14 through Chapter 17 of John's Gospel, Christ speaks of the Father by name, or refers to Him, a total of 122 times.[4] Clearly, the truth of the Father and His love is the essence of the *Discourse*, especially the part known since the sixteenth century as the *"High Priestly Prayer"* of Jesus.[5]

In His prayer, Christ's words are addressed directly to the Father rather than to the disciples, who overhear.[6] Although still present in the world, Jesus considers His earthly mission as a thing of the past.[7] Whereas He had previously stated that the Apostles could not follow Him, He now wishes for them to be in union with the Father too,[8] especially through the Father *consecrating* them in truth. Thus, as Jesus passes into eternity the world is now to be challenged by the mission of His disciples.[9] It is a mission to call mankind to the Father through the Son and the Spirit, the *Paraclete*, who Jesus promises to send to them.[10]

In essence, their challenge is more fully revealed to them; they are now *Apostles of the Most Holy Trinity*.

They must take to the world the *complete truth* of the revealed God, the truth given to them by Christ, the only begotten Son who was with His Father "before the world began" (Jn 17:24).

APOSTLES OF THE FATHER

Sparked by St. Phillip's request to see the Father, the *Last Discourse* is instrumental in understanding the mission of the Church. Jesus tells the Apostles that He and they are *consecrated* to the truth of the Father and that the Father's love for mankind needs to be heralded loud and clear and spread far and wide throughout the world.

To this very day, it has been Christ's message to us.

We are called to be *consecrated* in order to bring to the Father the honor and glory the world must come to see and know. As Christ called His Apostles, so must we answer the call of our God. We must, quite simply, tell the world of the Father's love and the depository of graces that He wishes to dispel upon mankind through His Divine Paternal Heart.

We must become consecrated *Apostles of the Father*.

We must be filled with love and zeal for our Father and consecrated in truth to Him like Jesus was. Indeed, although divine, Jesus would probably humbly declare Himself an Apostle of His Father too.

This is because His love and zeal for the Father were present in His every word and deed until His *Ascension* into heaven.

CHAPTER TWO

CONSECRATION TO OUR FATHER

"Anyone who loves me will be true to my word and my Father will love him; we will come to him and make our dwelling place with him"
(Jn 14-23).

Love is the inspiration for all that is done and beheld in heaven and on earth. It is God's legacy to us. It is what binds us to Him and to each other.

It is what constitutes the Family of God.[1]

God's children, therefore, are of consequence in His eyes. We are His beloved. We come from Him and are to return to Him – to His Divine Paternal Heart. Unfortunately, the true meaning of this truth has remained hidden. But now, its full importance must be realized; for our hearts are ready, as our world is ready, to return to the Father. And He is leading us to return to Him, to His home – *His Heart* – where He desires to delight in us for His holy purpose.

Now and always, our Father in heaven is but a heartbeat away from all His children. For our hearts are joined with His – and with that, His Fatherly love. His desire then, for our daily lives, is for each of His children to make the "choice" to be reunited with Him.

This is His holy and ordained will.

This is His plan for us.[2]

Thus, with the Rosary as our spiritual weapon to defeat the power of the Evil One in our lives and in the world, we must also continue to mend our separation from the Father and move towards His loving arms and Paternal Heart.

This can be better achieved by individuals giving themselves, through personal consecration to the Father, back to His Paternal Heart – where each and every soul is conceived in the Father's love.

WHAT IS CONSECRATION?

Adam and Eve's choice to disobey God's will in the Garden was first and foremost a decision in both their *minds* and *wills* before an action was undertaken. In essence, their wills rejected the Father's will. Thus, we can do what they did not: we can say "yes" to our Father's will, individually and collectively, in order for *us* to truly turn toward Him in a meaningful way.

While there are many ways to give ourselves to our Father, a personal act of consecration to Him is perhaps the best way to demonstrate such love for our Creator.

Consecration is a solemn dedication to a special person, place, or thing. In religious terms, it signifies one's total giving, the placing aside of all else in order to be completely in the service of God.

Moreover, to consecrate oneself means to set oneself apart from *evil*, to turn to the Lord , and be prepared to be used by Him. It means to associate with the *sacred* in order to grow towards God and His will for us. The Bible tells us, "Consecrate yourselves therefore, and be holy; for I am the Lord your God" (Lv 20:7).

TWO PARTS TO CONSECRATION

There are two parts to the process of consecrating ourselves to God: our part and God's part. Our part is first the practical side of removing ourselves from sinful living. We especially need to resist the temptation of "serious sin." We do this by applying our minds and hearts to what is *good, pure, and of God*. In essence, we try to become "less" of this world, although we still live in and must be a part of it.

Through consecration, we then draw near to God and His design for our life. And, with the help of the Sacraments, consecration helps become a spiritual roadmap for holy living – the drinking in of God's presence – every moment of our life. Thus, once on this path, we become even less attracted to this world and its charms. In this way, we seek God and His will, for as God's presence increases, sin and unwanted behavior are replaced by the joy and happiness that comes from greater purity of mind, body, heart, and soul.

Finally, consecration also helps find within us the desire to be righteous in the eyes of God, for it inspires a yearning to please Him like all children wish to please their earthly parents.

God's part in our consecration to Him is inherent in His desire to dwell in us; He wishes to draw near to our hearts, so that His love is something we can feel more and never want to be separated from again. God knows that His presence cleanses us and makes us holy, as He is holy, giving to us new life in every way. This is what God desires for every soul. Thus, through consecrating ourselves to our Father, He sees we desire Him too. Therefore, He knows that He is permitted to act in us, to change us, and make us more like Him.

THE OLD TESTAMENT

The Old Testament is clear that God had desired consecration from His chosen people:
- "Consecrate to me all the first-born; whatever is the first to open the womb

among the people of Israel, both of man
and of beast, is mine" (Ex 13:2).

- "And the Lord said to Moses, "Go to the
  people and consecrate them today and
  tomorrow, and let them wash their
  garments" (Ex 19:10).

- "So Moses went down from the mountain
  to the people, and consecrated the people;
  and they washed their garments" (Ex 19:14).

- "You shall be men consecrated to me;
  therefore you shall not eat any flesh that
  is torn by beast in the field; you shall
  cast it to the dogs" (Ex 22:31).

- "And he poured some of the anointing
  oil on Aaron's head, and anointed him,
  to consecrate him" (Lv 8:12).

- "And he said, 'Peaceably; I have come to
  sacrifice to the Lord; consecrate yourselves,
  and come with me to the sacrifice.' And he
  consecrated Jesse and his sons, and invited
  them to the sacrifice" (1 Sam 16:5).

- "O Lord, God of heaven, behold their arrogance,
  and have pity on the humiliation of our people,

and look this day upon the faces of those who are consecrated to thee" (Jth 6:19).

Moreover, while Scripture speaks of God's people consecrating themselves to the Lord, it also speaks of God Himself taking the initiative and consecrating His chosen ones, preparing them to undertake His holy plan for their lives:

- "For they had afflicted him; yet he had been consecrated in the womb as prophet, to pluck up and afflict and destroy, and likewise to build and to plant" (Sir 49:7).

- "Before I formed you in the womb I knew you, and before you were born I consecrated you; I appointed you a prophet to the nations" (Jer 1:5).

- "Be silent before the Lord God! For the day of the the Lord is at hand; the Lord has prepared a sacrifice and consecrated his guests" (Zep 1:7).

Indeed, from Samson to Samuel to Solomon, there are many chosen souls in the Old Testament who were consecrated by God in the womb or in early childhood – much like David, the anointed of God's Heart. This was God's way of establishing a special relationship with souls, so they could better come to know, love, and honor Him in their lives.

CHAPTER TWO

THE NEW TESTAMENT

In the New Testament, we especially take note that Scripture reveals how the Father "consecrated Jesus" before He came into the world:

> "Do you say of him whom the Father
> consecrated and sent into the world
> 'You are blaspheming,' because I said,
> 'I am the Son of God" (Jn 10:36)?

Likewise, Jesus consecrated Himself to His Father and encouraged the need for consecration. In what Scripture calls Christ's *Last Discourse*, He prayed to his Father for His Apostles to be consecrated:

> "Consecrate them by means of truth –
> 'Your word is truth.' As you have sent
> me into the world, so I have sent them
> into the world; I consecrate myself for
> their sakes now, that they may be
> consecrated in truth" (Jn 17:17-19).

To consecrate ourselves to the Father, therefore, is to consecrate ourselves in truth to His Paternal Heart. In essence, it is the path to unifying our heart with His Heart, so that like the Apostles, we can be totally of God.

CHAPTER THREE

A LADDER TO OUR FATHER'S HEART

*"Consecrate them by means of truth – 'Your word is truth.'
As you have sent me into the world, so I have sent them
into the world; I consecrate myself for their sakes now,
that they may be consecrated in truth" (Jn 17:17-19).*

As we see in the lives of God's Saints, individual consecration to our Father is the path to a new life in Him. It is the path that each of God's children should be encouraged to take, for it allows us to know our Father personally and to walk with Him in our daily life. It allows us to take His hand in trust, and escape a culture God did not desire for man to live in.

As life in ancient Rome was for the first Christians, our culture today breeds despair and crushes hopes and dreams. It is a culture that removes peace. Through consecration, therefore, God intervenes and holds us in the palm of His hand. In this way, though still in this world, we become closer to the Father's Heart, where He can cleanse us of the culture and bless our lives with goodness, hope, and love. In this way, we begin to make our way back home to Him and find His will for our lives.

To know, love and honor our Father is our calling. *Through* and *in* our Father, we are each called to His truth. Deep within our hearts, He will show us this truth when we are consecrated to Him and when we seek His divine will for our lives.

A BETTER WORLD

Warm and welcome in the Heart of our Father, our consecration to Him is a *ladder* to our Father's Heart and brings miracles into our lives and families. This is because we are filled with a brilliance that glimmers in the eyes of the souls of all who meet us. It is a spark of the divine, a *sign* of our Father's presence, in which those who meet us wish to possess and experience in their lives too.

Thus, consecration is an awakening, a time of personal renewal that can then lead us to a better world. The Father, strong and vital, is *Life*, the life inside us. When we choose to step into our Father's will, this *life* of His transforms us. We see and feel his glory and we take joy in our efforts to be part of Him. Like Jesus, who is *the Way, the Truth, and the Life*, we allow the life of Christ to take us into the Heart of our Father; here there is only love and peace, a oneness with Him that is priceless and incomparable to anything else the world has to offer.

"*Seek and ye shall find,*" Jesus tells us. Through consecration, we find our Father. We find His love for us, for all His children. Thus, we begin to lead the world back to Him. Together, united *to* and *with* Him, mankind can then begin to enter a new era, the *Era of Peace* promised at Fatima.

Past the pain, past the darkness of our times, an angelic army seeks to lead us into the new times, to help bridge for us the future that has been promised to mankind. It is a future where, comforted by Mary, we are no longer separated from our Father but sealed and carried in His love for us – secured safely in the *Ark of our Father's Heart* – where all darkness succumbs to His light and mankind is in more intimate union with its Creator.

A SPECIAL CONSECRATION PRAYER

How then should we consecrate ourselves to the Father?

Although there are prayers of consecration to God the Father that are good and acceptable, a beautiful eight-day octave prayer; one that includes meditations of both the Old and New Testament's mysteries, appears to have been inspired by the Holy Spirit for the times at hand.

Because of its exceptional content, I believe it is a devotion to the Father that perhaps the Church should examine and, if found worthy, encourage and promote some day. This is because it is a prayer that allows the faithful to say "*yes*" to our Father, to begin individually, one person at a time, to end our separation from Him in a special way.

The octave prayer entitled *God Our Father, Consecration and Feast Day for the Father of All Mankind (available from St. Andrew's Productions)*, outlines a path that a soul can undertake in a deliberate meditative action. It permits the consecration of one's self to God the Father over an eight-day period.

While the Church in its wisdom may seek to study and recommend changes to its present format, the eight-day consecration prayer has been acclaimed by theologians[1] and is perhaps a spiritual window into better understanding our need to return to God the Father in a meaningful, prayerful way – a way that is a purposeful step along the Church's path to the fulfillment of its mission in salvation history.[2]

CONSECRATION TO GOD OUR FATHER

The most compelling precedent for consecrating ourselves to God our Father over an eight-day period, or octave, is found in the *Gospel of St. John*, Chapter 10:22-39. This passage describes how Jesus, during the eight-day *Feast of Dedication*, reveals how He had been consecrated to God our Father (Jn 10:36)[3]

Jesus explains that He consecrated Himself to our Father so we, too, could be consecrated to Him in truth (cf. Jn 17:19-21).[4] The concept of consecration to God our Father is crucial because, as Jesus tells us, "the hour is coming, and now is, when the true worshippers will worship the Father in spirit and truth, for such the Father seeks to worship him. God is a spirit, and those who worship him must worship in spirit and truth" (Jn 4:23-24).[5] Thus, if we follow Jesus, if we model ourselves after Him, shouldn't we also consecrate ourselves to God our Father during an eight-day period, so that we, too, can adore Him "in spirit and in truth?"[6] Therefore, if we choose to consecrate ourselves to God Our Father, how should this be done?

The concept of an "octave," or eight-day feast, has been significant in our relationship with God since the beginning of our salvation history.[7] It is not by coincidence that Jesus chose to reveal His consecration to God our Father on the eight-day *Feast of the Dedication*. Clearly, the octave symbolizes a designated period of time in which God's children grow and His relationship with them changes or is transformed.[8]

Unlike other consecration methods, *The Holy Octave of Consecration to God Our Father* views the "big picture" of our salvation history.[9] It involves the entire process of our spiritual journey that progresses towards our Father, which includes the most prominent figures of our faith: Mary, our Mother; Jesus, our God and our Savior; and the Holy Spirit, our God and our Sanctifier – with progression always toward God our Father.[10]

PERIODS OF TRANSFORMATION

God's Word, in both the Old and New Testaments, provides us with extensive Scriptural support for an eight-day, or "octave," format. From the *Book of Genesis* to the Gospels and Epistles, the number "eight" is used to signify salvation, covenant, purification, and dedication.[11] Perhaps, more importantly, it is used to indicate the end of one era and the beginning of another in which God the Father is revealed, manifested, and is presented to His children in a special way.

Holy Scripture illustrates that in the past, these periods of transformation always involved a time of our turning away from God, a time of purification and cleansing, a time of re-dedication, and a time of regathering and renewal.[12]

The octave or eight-day period is significant, then, in representing a divinely ordained process that involves a shifting from one period to the next. Often the process that propels us from one period into the next has involved seven days of praise, thanksgiving, offering, and repentance, followed by an eighth day of solemnity and assembly of God's children.[13] This process can work on two levels to purify and dedicate us: individually and as a body. Therefore, *The Holy Octave of Consecration to God our Father* is necessary and much needed in these times – for each of us individually and for the Church as a whole.[14]

To place the need for consecration to God our Father in proper perspective for the times we live in, we should remember that at the turn of the last century, Pope Leo XIII dedicated the world to the Sacred Heart of Jesus.[15] Again in 1925, Pope Pius XI ordered a formal consecration of mankind to the Sacred Heart of Jesus, to be publicly recited and renewed annually on the Feast of Christ the King.[16]

THE FEAST OF THE FATHER

Finally, *the Holy Octave of Consecration to God Our Father* prayer, in its present format, is intended as a formal eight-day celebration for God our Father culminating with the feast day on the first Sunday of the "eighth" month, August.[17]

The solemn eighth day is celebrated under the title, *The Feast of the Father of All Mankind*, a special day that not only the Church would celebrate but the whole world, for there is only one Father of all mankind,[18] only one Father whose Paternal Heart the world must come to see and know, to love and honor in a special way. Indeed, for it is a Heart that wishes to now dwell in the temples of His children in the way, Scripture says, it once dwelled in Christ's Father's House, the great Temple of Jerusalem:

> "And now I have chosen and consecrated this house that my name be here forever; my eyes and my *Heart* also shall be there always" (2 Chr 7:16).

CHAPTER FOUR

THE SOLEMNITY OF THE DIVINE PATERNAL HEART

"A son honors his father, and servants their master; If, then, I am a Father, where is the honor due me?" (Mal 1:6)

Each of us is conceived in the Paternal Heart of God Our Father, and each of us is called to return to His Heart. Returning to our heavenly Father, to His Paternal Heart, is therefore what every soul desires and is inspired by grace to discover.

The desire to return to our Father is His gift to us, a *perfect gift*, for "[e]very best gift, and every perfect gift, is from above, coming down from the Father of lights" (Jas 1"17). But the call to know the Father, to know the Heart of the Father, is more than just a call to experience a greater personal relationship with Him. In truth, it is a call to the Church, the world, and mankind to come to the

Father. It is a historic passage of faith and time, intended to bring hope to men and nations that they may live in peace and security along the path of salvation.

It is the long awaited fulfillment of the Church's call to make the Father known just as He is – so that mankind may increase its trust and love for its heavenly Father, a Father who desires to watch over and delight in His children like a painter contemplating the picture He has painted, for mankind is the masterpiece of our Father's creation.

In essence, the Spirit's call in the *New Evangelization* is a call for each soul to return through Christ to its Father so that He can shower His love upon all and heal our wounds and so we then can pay homage to our Father in a way that is deserving of Him, for He is "one God and Father of all, who is above all and through all and in all" (Eph 4:6).

But there needs to be more.

The Church needs to acknowledge the cry of God's children – their cry of love in response to the Spirit's invitation – by proclaiming a *Feast for God Our Father*. It is to be the *Feast of Life*:

The Solemnity of the Divine Paternal Heart:
The Feast of the Father of All Mankind

According to theologians, such a feast would lead to many positive benefits for all of humanity and would fulfill *Lumen Gentium's* prophetic words: "In Christ, the head of all things, all honor and glory may be rendered to the Creator, the Father of the universe."[1] Indeed, the *Feast of the Father of All Mankind* would most of all fulfill the need to bring honor and glory to God our Father, and to finally answer the cries of God's children that have echoed throughout the centuries.

It is a cry that will go on until this need is fulfilled, for such honoring of our Father is long overdue; it is an honor that is encouraged and presaged in many passages in Scripture, such as in the *Book of Sirach*:

> "For the Lord sets a father in honor
> over his children
> and confirms a mother's authority over her sons.
> Those who honor their father
> atone for sins;
> They store up riches who respect their mother.
> Those who honor their father will
> have joy in their own children,
> and when they pray they are heard.
> Those who respect their father
> will live a long life;
> Those who obey the Lord honor their mother…
> Kindness to a father will not be forgotten;
> it will serve as a sin offering – it will take lasting root" (Sir 3:2-6, 14).

CHAPTER FIVE

THE FEAST OF THE FATHER OF ALL MANKIND

"'Father, glorify your name.' Then a voice came from heaven, 'I have glorified it and will glorify it again" (Jn 12:28).

In the crucifixion, death, and resurrection of Christ, a great mystery of His teachings emerged. A new form of worship and a new Temple was meant to be built, replacing the old form of worship and the old Temple. In Jesus' words, "Destroy this sanctuary, and in three days I'll raise it up" (Jn 2:19), the promise of the ages reveals its coming fruition.[1]

Christ's Resurrection assures us that His Father, the Father of creation and mankind, is finally to be recognized, praised and honored as the one, true God; replacing centuries of pagan worship and even the monotheistic form of Jewish worship. The most Holy Trinity, revealed by Christ as the real God, now would have real followers who worship in *truth*. And the risen Savior's words to Mary of Magdala center this worship on the Father: "I am going to my Father and your Father, to my God and your God" (Jn 20:17).

Thus, this new, divine worship is to be forever addressed and focused on the Father, for it is the *path of truth* as "commanded by the Father" (2 Jn:4), who Christ sought to lift all mankind towards, by way of His Ascension, to the *Father's right hand* [2] (Mk 16:19).

THE NEW WORSHIP

This higher truth had already been foretold, in no uncertain terms, to the Samaritan woman at the well. Christ had assured her that *"the hour is coming, and is now, when true worshipers will worship the Father 'in spirit and truth,' for the Father is seeking such people to worship him"* (Jn 4:21-23).[3]

With Christ's reply to the Samaritan woman, the age of the past is forever over, the past the woman spoke of and believed was centered on the teachings of *"our ancestors who worshipped on this mountain"* (Jn 4:20). Now, the Trinity was revealed. Jesus spoke of "God Himself, our Father" (1 Thes 3:11), the one Father of all mankind, who was truly our Father, who *loved* His children , and who, therefore, deserved to be worshiped not out of fear or out of *tradition,* but out of love in return.[4]

The new worship, addressed to the Person of the Father, inspired by the Holy Spirit, and revealed by Christ, implies a newly perceived relationship between creature and Creator. It is a relationship founded on love, as the humble obedient creature, God's friend (cf. Jn 15:15), has found "love in God the Father" (cf. Jude 1:1) – a love so great and transforming that it causes the creature to have desire to not only love the Creator with a heartfelt need, but also have desire to honor and glorify Him, for it finds no better way to fulfill this *heart to Heart* relationship. Like the ancient Israelites, the creature desires to stand before his God, his heavenly Father and cry:

"Blessed be your glorious name, which is exalted above all blessing and praise" (Neh 9:5).

THE HOLY LITURGY

In no uncertain terms, this *honoring of the Father*, this "work of truth" (Jn 3:7), is already addressed in the Holy Liturgy. From the beginning, the Church had established that all liturgical worship must be directed to the Father. The *Catechism of the Catholic Church* states the Father is the source and goal of the Liturgy.[5] In the Liturgy, God the Father is blessed and adored as the *origin* of all the blessings of creation and salvation, with which He has given us in His Son in order to give us the Spirit of filial adoption.[6] In the New Covenant, all prayer is the loving relationship of God's children with their Father – who is good beyond measure – with His Son, Jesus Christ, and with the Holy Spirit.

Some may ask, if all liturgical worship and all Christian prayer either directly or indirectly is addressed to the Father, is there truly a need for the inauguration of a special feast in honor of God Our Father? And is this need not already met with the *Feast of the Blessed Trinity*?

These questions and objections, along with others, have been pondered since the seventeenth century, when documented efforts to establish a liturgical feast for God the Father first began to be recorded.[7]

EARLY EFFORTS TO INAGURATE A FEAST OF THE FATHER

In 1657, Pope Alexander VII received a petition from Leige, Belgium requesting approbation of a Divine Office and Mass in honor of the Eternal Father. The Sacred Congregation of Rite refused to grant it on December 1, 1657.[8] In 1684, King Charles II of Spain pursued the same efforts with no success. Over the next two centuries, similar efforts produced the same results. Pope Leo XIII, in 1897, was the last pope to note the cause briefly alluding to it in his encyclical letter on the Holy Spirit, *Divinum Illud*, although not attempting doctrinal examination of the issue.[9]

For the most part, the objections have emphasized the lack of precedent in regards to feasts intended to venerate the individual Persons of the Holy Trinity. In addition, there became a concern for the potential excessive multiplication of feasts that would come if a feast of the Father was implemented, as well as potential theological problems – such as confusion over the divine essence of the Trinity, or the false assumption of each divine Person with their own feast having several divine natures attributed to them. Some argued that since no such feast for the Father has ever been inaugurated, the example of the "wisdom of the ancients" needs to be followed.[10]

Nevertheless, throughout the twentieth century, efforts to promote a feast for the Father have continued to surface.[11] Various petitions have been attempted and, in the latter part of the century, eminent theologians, religious, and laity have taken up the cause by lending their authoritative voices through writings and lectures.[12] Collectively, these individuals believe that the objections of the past, for the most part, are not insurmountable and that the time has come for the Church to inaugurate a feast in honor of God Our Father.

They especially emphasize that the Church, now two thousand years old, does not in any way honor the Creator, God Our Father, with a special day. And this, they argue, is in itself most surprising and unacceptable, and that it should be addressed at this time in history.[13]

HONORING THE FATHER'S LOVE

Although the need for the Church to confront the inauguration of separate feasts in honor of the individual Persons of the Trinity is perhaps a matter to be taken up and addressed at some point – considering the breadth and depth of the theological questions involved in such an undertaking – any action forthcoming can be seen as most probably in the distant future.

However, in lieu of the Church's institution of many feasts in honor of the attributes, traits, and divine actions of both the Son and the Spirit – such as the Feasts of *Pentecost*, the *Sacred Heart of Jesus*, the *Precious Blood* and most recently Christ's *Divine Mercy* – an effort to inaugurate a feast in honor of the Father's divine paternal love as seen in His Paternal Heart presents sound reason for immediate action, acceptance, and approval in both theological and practical terms. Moreover, it would uphold and be consistent with the precedent established by existing feasts that honor the divine traits and characteristics of Christ and the Holy Spirit; at the same time, it would be the easiest way to confront and place aside the objections of the past.

Let us, therefore, consider the many reasons why it is time to honor and glorify our Father's Divine Paternal Heart in a special way, why it is time to "rejoice in the Lord" (Heb 3:18), and why it is time "to sing to the glory of his name" (Ps 66:2), as we read in Scripture that God's faithful are called to do:

- "A son honors his father, and a servant his master; if then I am a Father, where is the honor due to me?" (Mal 1:6).

- "Blessed art thou, O Lord the God of our fathers; and worthy to be praised, and glorified, and exalted above all forever: and blessed is the holy name of thy glory: and worthy to be praised, and exalted above all in all ages" (Dn 3:52).

- "Worthy are you, Lord our God, to receive glory and honor and power" (Rv 4:11).

- "Worship him who made heaven and earth and sea and springs of water" (Rv 14:6-7).

- "Father, glorify thy name. A voice therefore came from heaven; I have glorified it, and will glorify it again" (Jn 12:28).

CHAPTER FIVE

"Worship him who made heaven and earth and sea and springs of water" (Rev 14:6-7).

Father, glorify thy name. A voice therefore came from heaven: I have glorified it, and will glorify it again (Jn 12:28).

CHAPTER SIX

THE CELEBRATION OF LIFE

> *"...he sent the people back to their tents, rejoicing and glad at heart for the good things the Lord had done for David, for Solomon, and for his people Israel" (2 Chr 7:10).*

First and foremost, a feast in honor of God our Father's Paternal Heart would express homage to His Fatherhood, especially His paternal love as expressed in Scripture (Eph 1:3-5) and manifested in the works of creation and salvation. Moreover, such a feast would invoke the works of Christ, who called upon us to *know* God the Father was *His* Father and our Father. A feast would truly do this, thereby renewing in a special way the faithful's confidence in the *Lord's Prayer* – particularly the prayer's essential them of loving our Father, the echo of Scripture's words as heard in the teachings of the prophets and recorded in the *First Commandment*: "To love God with all our heart, mind and strength."[1]

Equally important, a feast for our Father would especially call to mind His *divinity*, His holiness, His awesomeness as God, and the giver of all gifts to His children through His omnipotent will and loving Paternal Heart. Indeed, a feast would "proclaim to all God's great power" (2 Mc 3:34).

THE GIVER OF LIFE

Some have argued in the past that this is accomplished in the liturgical *Feast of the Blessed Trinity*. However, theologians today point out that this feast calls for homage to the Trinity's *unity in nature*, and does not express homage to the Father or the divine Fatherhood – especially His divine paternal love as is manifested in the work of creation and salvation in relation to the members of the human race. For the most part, a feast in honor of the Paternal Heart of the Father would truly commemorate that our Father is a loving Father, the *Giver of Life*, whom we attribute our existence to in a loving and thankful way.

In essence, it would be the *Celebration of Life*. In turn, the mystery of the Son's Incarnation would be renewed too, as Christians see the need to be united with the Father, just as was the Son in the flesh. Similarly, it would renew our relationship with the Holy Spirit, for in honoring our Father, the Spirit imparts in our souls that the image of the Son we are called to see is *one with the Father*.[2]

Especially for the laity, a feast in honor of our Father would emphasize our need to see and glorify His name in a more enlightened way; this would cause the faithful, some of whom that may have had a *fear of the Father*, to deeply penetrate through meditation the truth of the Father of all mankind and His great love for each and every soul.[3] Through such meditation, the call to seek heaven and be with our Father forever would fill people's hearts, giving greater reality to life's most important purpose and calling.[4] Indeed, it is a calling to our "ABBA" in trust and not fear, as we reach up to take His hand in order to be led into his Kingdom forever, and to return to His Divine Paternal Heart, where we first were conceived.[5] This is the mystery of Himself the Father is calling us to know. St. John Paul II writes, "Did not Christ say that our Father who 'sees in secret,' is always waiting for us to have recourse to him in every need and always wanting for us to study his mystery: the mystery of the Father and his love?"[6]

HUMAN FATHERHOOD

In the tradition of the many feasts in honor of Christ, Mary, and the Saints, a feast for our Father would also celebrate an important phase in the mystery of salvation in each year of the liturgical cycle.[7]

The Father's plan, which leads the Church and governs the Liturgy, would be expressed with greater clarity each year. This would mean that the solemnity of the mystery of the Father and His paternal love, as symbolized in His Divine Paternal Heart, would be similar to the cultural development of *Father's Day* (a celebration that occurs in many nations around the world) and would become a highlight of the liturgical cycle, casting great light on divine Fatherhood in relationship to the significance of human fatherhood and its deserving of honor.[8] In this light, we would consider heaven and earth to be more closely united and seen with a new strength of bonding through the fullest meaning of the virtue of fatherhood, which contains mercy and forgiveness in its love.[9]

In addition, today's families would be enhanced through such a celebration with not only the greater ongoing reality of the Fatherhood of God, but of motherhood and the love between the spouses. This is because the example of the Father's paternal love would also have a profound influence on the home and the need for authority, respect, and love in all situations. Simply stated, the example of the Father's paternal love would reinforce the idea that a family must persevere in hope and faith.[10] According to St. John Paul II, all of this is "fundamental to....the *civilization of love*... [because] the family is organically linked to this civilization."[11]

PROFOUND EUMENICAL IMPLICATIONS

From a strictly theological perspective, a feast for God our Father's Paternal Heart contains many ecumenical implications because of its sound Scriptural roots. The fundamental truth emphasized at the beginning of the *Letter to the Ephesians* (Eph 1:2-14) is that salvation is governed by the Father's intention, in and through Christ, to establish His universal Fatherhood.[12] This implies that our Father is not only to be understood as *universal Father*, but also as the individual Father of each and every human being. Such a feast would express this awareness with clarity.[13]

Furthermore, Catholics and Christians of every denomination throughout the world could relive the mystery of salvation in its various states and in its most important events each year. This is because our Father is at the beginning and at the conclusion of this mystery.[14] Therefore, the entire process of sanctification results from our Father's paternal love, His Paternal Heart, which is primordial and decisive; therefore, deserves to be recognized and honored by a special feast.[15]

ONE COMMON FATHER

Lastly, such a feast would be also more than a celebration on the Catholic liturgical calendar. The creation of a feast in honor of God our Father's Paternal Heart would espouse profound ecumenical implications and be a basis for unity of all Christians and all human beings, for our Father – the one and only Father – embraces all His children in His Fatherly love and in His Divine Paternal Heart.[16]

Consequently, like common Christian celebrations, including Christmas and Easter, and also like our common patrimony in the *Our Father* prayer, a feast for our Father could come to be shared by all Christian denominations and wherever the sanctity of human fatherhood is held in respect and honor. This is because the joy of finding God, manifested in many religious as *one common Father*, would be an inspiration for every person and for every heart everywhere.[17]

Once more, we are reminded of the prophetic words of Pope Benedict XVI: "Christians long for the entire human family to call upon God as *'Our Father!'*"[18], an echo of St. John Paul II's call in his apostolic letter, *Euntes in Mundum*, for there "to be one family of God on earth."¹⁹

CHAPTER SEVEN

RAISING OUR VOICES TO THE FATHER

"Honor God and give him glory, for his time has come to sit in judgment. Worship the Creator of heaven and earth..."(Rv 14:7).

With all of this in mind, such a great and glorious feast, as I already noted, deserves to be inaugurated and celebrated in the tradition of an *octave,* the practice of celebrating a major feast on the feast day itself and for seven days preceding or seven days thereafter.[1]

This practice began in the Old Testament tradition of prolonging a feast day such as the feast of *Passover* and *Tabernacles* (cf. 1 Mc 4:56). Today, it is continued in the Church, primarily at Christmas and Easter. For all Christians, an octave celebration would involve eight days of prayer, Scriptural readings, meditation, and (for Catholics) participation in the Holy Mass, the Eucharist, and Sacrament of Reconciliation; this period of time is culminated with the feast day, which could also be a day of individual consecration (*and then each year a renewal of such consecration*) to the Father and His Paternal Heart.[2]

In this tradition, *The Solemnity of the Divine Paternal Heart of God Our Father: The Feast of the Father of All Mankind*, would be an annual eight-day celebration beginning and ending with complete attention to our Father; we note that this occurred in the life of Christ Himself, whose first recorded words in Scripture focused us on the Father: "[D]id you not know, that I must be about my Father's business?" (Lk 2:49) as were those among the last from His lips on the Cross, "Father, into your hands I commend my spirit" (Lk 23:46).

This glorious tradition of honoring God our Father has already been adopted annually by many in the Catholic Church in the Philippines, where an octave of celebration with individual consecration culminating on the feast day, the *Feast of the Father of all Mankind*, is celebrated on the first Sunday in August every year.[3]

RAISING OUR VOICES IN PRAYER

Therefore, through the powerful intercession of Mary, *The Mother of All Mankind*, "who prays for the unity of the Family of God,"[4] the world is called to return to its Father, *The Father of All Mankind*, who is supreme good, who is our fortress and deliverer, who is the giver and keeper of all *life*, and who is *our Father*.

Now, in reflection of their Mother's total *fiat*, Mary's children unite in their total *fiat* to their Father's Paternal Heart, saying *yes* to *life* and giving the Father what He desires most: the praise, honor, and glory that is rightfully and deservingly His, so that He can cover the world with His grace and mercy, so He can *come down* to rescue His children from their errant ways, and so He can reveal His great love for His children at this moment in time by bringing the *civilization of life* into the world with one sweeping wave of His mighty hand!

Through consecration of ourselves, our nations, and our world by the bishops and the Pope to the Divine Paternal Heart of God the Father, through the declaration of a solemn feast day in the universal Church in honor of our Father, humanity can build a new world, departing forever the shores of today's dark age and arriving at last in a new and glorious epoch of human history.

ST. JOHN PAUL II

Thus, in St. John Paul II's prophetic words, the prayer of our hearts storms heaven like the crashing peel of the rams' horn upon the walls of Jericho: "[W]e raise our voices and pray that the love which is in the Father may once again be revealed at this stage of history , and that through the work of the Son and Holy Spirit, it may be shown to be present in our modern world to be more powerful than evil: more powerful than sin and death."[5]

Indeed, the time has come for our blessed Father, the comforter of man to help His children carry their crosses of redemption so that the world will see the era of reconciliation with God and the coming of the foretold *Era of Peace* promised by Mary at Fatima. It is to be an era of love, joy and peace on earth – delivered from the Immaculate Heart of Mary to the Divine Paternal Heart of God Our Father.

CHAPTER EIGHT
APOSTLES OF THE FATHER

"Did you not know, that I must be about my Father's business" (Lk 2:49)?

In our world today, the *Father of Life* is truly the answer to the *Culture of Death*. Therefore, our Father – the one and only Father – is ready to help us confront and defeat this great crisis of our time.

And He will bring this victory through His children. We need merely to *consecrate* ourselves to Him and let Him work in and through us. We need to hold the Father's standard high and go into battle with Him leading the way.

But more importantly, the time has come for mankind to realize it has been separated from its Father for too long and needs to return to Him. This truth, this reality, must become visible in the world through those who are ready to become

His special followers and lead the world back to Him. We must lead the Father's children back to Him through His Word and His Spirit – through His one, holy, Catholic and Apostolic Church.

A CALL TO THE LAITY

This is a call to the religious and the laity, who through inspired efforts must take the truth of the Father to their parishioners and fellow religious, to their friends and neighbors, to all they know and meet in their daily lives. While religious orders for priests and nuns in the Father's name will arise, along with holy and blessed Sacramentals such a medals and scapulars of Him, so must come new conferences, organizations, hospitals, schools and churches in the Father's name. These are the efforts we must work hard to bring into existence in the tradition of our Catholic forefathers, those who filled the world with churches and Church institutions in Christ's name and the names of the great saints of the past.

Moreover, we must also take to the highway, especially today's super highway of information, which is more than capable of communicating the reality of our Father to an infinite number of people. Using today's technology and social media prowess, God our Father can now be brought into the homes of millions of believers and non-believers alike. As the Angels behold in heaven, a concentrated and determined effort to make the *Face of the Father* visible to all mankind must come.[1]

CHAPTER EIGHT

THE FATHER WILL LEAD US

With confidence, we can trust the Father Himself will answer the prayers of those who seek His creative guidance and divine assistance in this work. Thus, in just a short period of time, I believe such efforts will bear great fruit. Countless numbers will consecrate themselves to the Father and because of their efforts, the Church will proclaim His Feast – *the Feast of the Divine Paternal Heart of God Our Father*!

After this, the *deluge* will then come; billions of God's children will seek their Father in order to know, love and honor Him in a greater way than ever before in history.

From my faith and experience, I suspect that many of the Father's chosen disciples are already in the world. Through His divine plan, God has seeded the ground and is already watering it with His tears of love for the work at hand.

Are you ready to be one of them?

THE CALL OF THE AGES

Over time, all has been working towards this end. The Father's appeal to His children, to all Israel, has remained constant. 'Come home,' He says, 'realize and be enlightened of My presence in your heart and in the world. Hear the words of My Shepherd, My Son Jesus, who calls to you from the Cross, to follow Him home to Me, back home to My HEART.'

Much awaits the *Family of God* in and through the Divine Paternal Heart of its Father.

The call of the ages has been sounded again in these times.
The peace of God descends on the *Apostles of the Father*, who are called to be about their *Father's business*, who are called to lead mankind forward to claim their true inheritance as sons and daughters of their Most High Father.

Consecration Prayer to *God Our Father*

My Dearest Father, please accept this offering of myself – my body, mind and soul:

I *praise* You for Your creation – all Your works and wonders.

I *thank* You for giving me life and for all that You have done for me.

I *offer* up to You all that You have so generously given me.

I am sincerely *sorry* for not knowing, loving, serving and honoring You as I should.

I embrace my *inheritance* as Your child, both the joy and the responsibilities.

I give you my **'Yes'** so that I may be an instrument of Your will.

I pledge my *fidelity* and I ask for the grace of steadfastness and perseverance in my faith.

Most loving, caring, and merciful of Fathers, in Your divine presence, I sincerely proclaim my love for You; I give myself (and my family) to You; and I solemnly consecrate myself (and my family) to You – now and forever.

Dearest Father, as Your child, I ask –

That You send Mary to guide me to Jesus, and that Jesus sends me the Holy Spirit so that they may all bring me to you.

That You dwell with me and in me – a living temple prepared by Mary, dedicated by Jesus, and purified by your Holy Spirit. And may I always be with You and in You.

That You permit me, as Your child, to be Your true and intimate friend – one who loves You above all things.

And that You come for me when I die, to bring me home to You.

I further ask You, Father, for the sake of all mankind:

To have mercy on all Your children – past, present, and future.

To bring peace to the world and to gather all Your children to Yourself.

And that Your Kingdom comes and Your will is done on earth as it is in heaven.

Amen.

PETITION FOR:
The Solemnity of the Divine Paternal Heart
The Feast of the Father of All Mankind

Your Holiness:

With humility and love, we, the children of God, petition you, the Vicar of Christ, to approve a Feast for God Our Father. We ask that this feast be entitled **The Solemnity of the Divine Paternal Heart – The Feast of the Father of All Mankind**, the eighth solemn day of the holy octave of consecration to God our Father. We ask that it be celebrated annually on the first Sunday of August. We believe that it is our privilege and responsibility to know, love, serve and honor God Our Father through such a yearly feast. We pray that Jesus our God and Savior, The Holy Spirit our God and Sanctifier, and Mary, our Mother, guide you in approving this octave feast so that all mankind may offer their "fiat" to God Our Father, and so that "His Kingdom comes and His will is done on earth as it is in heaven."

Respectfully Submitted:

Name (Signature)	ADDRESS
1._____	_____
	_____
2._____	_____
3._____	_____
	_____
4._____	_____
	_____
5._____	_____
	_____

PLEASE COPY AND DISTRIBUTE THIS PETITION
Mail all petitions to the following address:

St. Andrew's Productions
PO Box 54204, Pittsburgh, PA 15244

Phone: 412-787-9735   Fax 412-787-5204

NOTES

INTRODUCTION

1. John Paul II, Encyclical Letter, *Tertio Millennio Adveniente*, IV, N. 49.
2. Ibid., IV, N. 54.
3. Jn 14:23.
4. John Paul II, Encyclical Letter, *Tertio Millennio Adveniente*, I, N. 7, N.8.
5. Ps 33:11.
6. Lk 15:11-31.
7. John R. Willis, S.J., *The Teachings of the Church Fathers*, San Francisco: Ignatius Press, 2002, pg. 185.
8. Johannes Quasten, *Patrology, Vol I, The Beginnings of Patristic Literature*, Allen, Texas: Christian Classics, 1952, pg. 240.
9. Paul Milcent, *Saint John Eudes*, Glasgow, England,: John S. Burns & Sons, 1963, pg. 130.
10. John K. Ryan (ed.), *Introduction to the Devout Life – St. Francis de Sales*, Garden City, New York: Image Books, 1972, pg 104.
11. *Divine Mercy in My Soul, The Diary of Sister M. Faustina Kowalska*, Stockbridge, Mass: 1987, N. 1270, pg.461.
12. Pius XII, Encyclical Letter, *Haurietis Aquas*, (15 May 1956), N. 106.
13. John Paul II, *Tertio Millennio Adveniente*, I, N. 7, N.8.
14. Joseph Ratzinger, Pope Benedict XVI, *Jesus of Nazareth, From the Baptism in the Jordan to the Transfiguration*, San Francisco: Ignatius Press, 2007, pp. 340-341.
15. *Catechism of the Catholic Church*, New Hope, Kentucky: Urbit et Orbi Communications, 1994, N.758.
16. Mal 2:10.
17. Rv 14:6-7.
18. 2 Chron 7:8-9.
19. Rv 14:6-7.
20. Raniero Cantalamessa, O.F.M. Cap., *Life in the Lordship of Christ: A Commentary on Paul's Epistle to the Romans*, New York: Sheed & Ward, 1990, pp. 96-97.
21. Jean Galot, *ABBA, Father, We Long to See Your Face – Insights into the First Person of the Trinity*, New York: Alba House, 1992, pp. 205-232.

CHAPTER ONE
ST. PHILIP AND THE FATHER

1. *The New American Bible*, Fireside Family Edition (1984-1985), Witchita, Kansas: Catholic Bible Publishers, 1970, pp. 1071-1072.
2. Mt 17:5.
3. Michael O'Carroll, C.S.Sp., *Trinitas, A Theological Encyclopedia of the Holy Trinity*, Collegeville, Minnesota: The Liturgical Press, 1987, pp. 136-137.
4. Author's personal commentary of the *Last Discourse*.
5. *The New American Bible*, footnote commentary by editors of *The Gospel According to John*, Chapter 17:1-26, pg. 1075.

6. Ibid.
7. Ibid.
8. Ibid.
9. Ibid.
10. Ibid.

CHAPTER TWO
CONSECRATION TO OUR FATHER

1. *Catechism of the Catholic Church*, N. 541, 542, 959
2. Ibid., N. 757, 758.

CHAPTER THREE
A LADDER TO OUR FATHER'S HEART

1. *Holy Octave of Consecration of God Our Father*, pp. III-IV.
2. Ibid.
3. Ibid., pg. 3.
4. Ibid.
5. Ibid.
6. Ibid.
7. Ibid.
8. Ibid.
9. Ibid.
10. Ibid.
11. Ibid.
12. Ibid.
13. Ibid.
14. Ibid.
15. Ibid.
16. Ibid.
17. Ibid.
18. Ibid.

CHAPTER FOUR
THE SOLEMNITY OF THE DIVINE PATERNAL HEART

1. Vatican Council II, *The Conciliar and Post Conciliar Documents, (28) The Dogmatic Constitution of the Catholic Church, Vatican II Lumen Gentium*, (21 November 1964), II, The People of God, pg. 369.

CHAPTER FIVE
THE FEAST OF THE FATHER OF ALL MANKIND

1. Jean Galot, S.J., *ABBA Father, We Long to See Your Face – Theological Insights into the First Person of the Trinity*, pp. 203-205.
2. Ibid.

3. Ibid., pg. 204.
4. Ibid.
5. *Catechism of the Catholic Church*, N. 1076, 1077, 1082.
6. Ibid. N. 1082.
7. Jean Galot, S.J., *ABBA Father, We Long to See Your Face – Theological Insights into the First Person of the Trinity*, pg. 206.
8. Ibid.
9. Leo XIII, Encyclical Letter, *Divinum Illud*, (4 May 1897).
10. Jean Galot, S.J., *ABBA Father, We Long to See Your Face – Theological Insights into the First Person of the Trinity*, pp. 207-212.
11. Thomas W. Petrisko (Ed.), *Queen of Peace Newspaper, God the Father Edition*, Mckees Rocks, Pennsylvania, St. Andrew's Productions, 1999.
12. Ibid.
13. Ibid.

CHAPTER SIX
THE CELEBRATION OF LIFE

1. Jean Galot, S.J., *ABBA Father, We Long to See Your Face – Theological Insights into the First Person of the Trinity*, pp. 203-232.
2. Ibid.
3. Ibid.
4. Ibid.
5. Ibid.
6. John Paul II, *Dives in Misericordia*, 1,2.
7. Jean Galot, S.J., *ABBA Father, We Long to See Your Face – Theological Insights into the First Person of the Trinity*, pp. 203-232.
8. Ibid.
9. Ibid.
10. Ibid.
11. John Paul II, *Letter to the Families from Pope John Paul II*, I, N. 13.
12. Jean Galot, S.J., *ABBA Father, We Long to See Your Face – Theological Insights into the First Person of the Trinity*, pp. 203-232.
13. Ibid.
14. Ibid.
15. Ibid., pp. 207-232
16. Ibid, pp. 215-232.
17. Ibid., pp. 206-232.
18. Benedict XVI, *Caritas in Veritate*, Conclusion, N. 79.
19. John Paul II, Apostolic Letter, *Euntes in Mundum*, (25 January 1988).

CHAPTER SEVEN
RAISING OUR VOICES TO THE FATHER

1. *The Holy Octave of Consecration to God Our Father*, McKees Rocks, Pennsylvania: St. Andrew's Productions, 1998.
2. Ibid.

3. Ricardo J. Cardinal Vidal, Chancery, Cardinal Rosales Pastoral Center, *Solemn Feast of the Father of All Mankind Newsletter and Homily*, (13 June 2006), 6000 Cebu City, Philippines.
4. John Paul II, Apostolic Letter, *Euntes in Mundum*, VI, N. 16.
5. John Paul II, *Dives in Misericordia*, VIII, N. 15.

CHAPTER EIGHT
APOSTLES OF THE FATHER

1. Mt 18-10.

Order at saintandrew.com

Now Available:

The Mystery of the Divine Paternal Heart of God Our Father

Dr. Thomas W. Petrisko

The great apostle of God the Father, Thomas Petrisko, has written a masterful theological and spiritual treatise to promote devotion to the *Paternal Heart of the Father* that will hopefully lead up to a special Feast for God the Father. You will, in this presentation, find all of the other powerful truths of our faith that flow from God the Father. In fact, every truth of life and holiness comes from the Father through the Son through the workings of the Holy Spirit. The time has come for us to acknowledge the role of God the Father, and to realize that he who has seen Jesus and His Sacred Heart, has also seen the Father and His Paternal Heart.

– Fr. William McCarthy, MSA,
April 12, 2013

Order at saintandrew.com

Now Available:

Living in the Heart of the Father
Dr. Thomas W. Petrisko

Jesus came to reveal that the God who "so loved the world that he gave his only Son" (Jn 3:16) had a Heart – a Divine Paternal Heart – the Heart of a Father who existed from eternity. Yes, the Divine Paternal Heart of the Father is the treasure of Heaven that desires to 'beat in unison' with our hearts through shared love in order that "Your kingdom come, your will be done on earth as {it is] in heaven" (Mt 6:10)Now, Dr. Thomas Petrisko sheds light on this infinite mystery of the Father to be known, loved and honored by each of his children , in this grace-filled 'era of time.' He also calls for a Feast Day in honor of the Divine Paternal Heart of God the Father. This Feast Day will help us to see with *'the eyes of our souls'* – to experience the love of our Father in the depths of our spiritual heart and to return to Him as His prodigal children, to return to the "God and Father of all, who is over all and through all and in all" (Eph 4:4-6).

– Father David Tourville, Feast of Christ the King, November 25, 2013

ABOUT THE AUTHOR

Dr. Thomas W. Petrisko was the President of the Pittsburgh Center for Peace from 1990 to 1998 and he served as the editor of the Center's ten *Special Edition Queen of Peace* newspapers. These papers, primarily featuring the apparitions and revelations of the Virgin May, were published in many millions and distributed throughout the world. In 1996, he founded St. Andrew's Productions, and in 1998, he founded the Father of All Mankind Apostolate.

He is the author of over 25 books, including: *The Fatima Prophecies, At the Doorstep of the World; The Face of the Father, An Exclusive Interview with Barbara Centilli Concerning her Revelations and Visions of God the Father; Glory to the Father, A Look at the Mystical Life of Georgette Faniel; For the Soul of the Family; The Story of the Apparitions of the Virgin Mary to Estela Ruiz; The Sorrow , the Sacrifice and the Triumph; The Visions, Apparitions and Prophecies of Christina Gallagher; Call of the Ages; The Prophecy of Daniel; In God's Hands,The Miraculous Story of Little Audrey Santo; Mother of the Secret; False Prophets of Today; St. Joseph and The Triumph of the Saints, The Last Crusade; The Kingdom of Our Father; Inside Heaven and Hell; Inside Purgatory; The Miracle of the Illumination; Fatima's Third Secret Explained; Living in the Heart of the Father; The Mystery of the Divine Paternal Heart of God Our Father and St. Philip and the Apostles of the Father.*

Dr. Petrisko, along with his wife Emily, have four daughters, Maria, Sarah, Natasha, Dominique and two sons, Joshua and Jesse.